Conceptualism

Conceptualism

Mind body & Art

Chavanese Wint

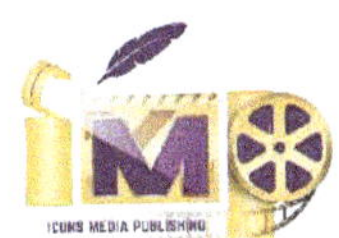

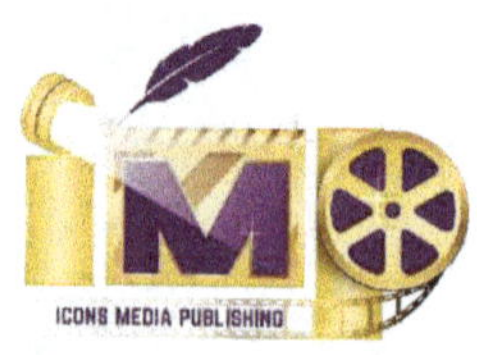
ICONS MEDIA PUBLISHING

Contents

DEDICATION

This book is a testament to the unwavering dedication of those who refuse to be confined by their current circumstances. It is for the dreamers who persistently pursue their goals, despite facing countless obstacles along the way. In a world filled with negativity and naysayers, this book serves as a beacon of hope and encouragement. It reminds us that we have the power within us to overcome any challenges and achieve the success we desire.

People who say 'IT' cannot be done,
Should never interfere with those who've begun,
For when you doubt and speak so low,
You'll only fuel their determination to grow.

~

Whatever I want in my life, I'll fight,
No matter the obstacles or height,
My choices are mine, not yours to choose,
So don't try and hold me back with your negative views.

~

If you continue with your negativity,
Trying to stop my creativity,
Just know that you will surely lose,
I won't let your words make me refuse.

~

My success depends on how I strive,
Not on your words trying to deprive,
So when you call me a failure,
I'll keep rising with unwavering valour.

~

For I already have the best job in the land,
And nothing can change that, understand?
Your negative behaviour won't bring me down,
For my faith and determination will always abound.

Success is not just measured by personal accomplishments, but rather by the impact one has on others. It's about guiding individuals away from destructive paths, motivating them to utilize their intellect, and assisting them in making wise choices. Moreover, success entails alleviating their hardships and struggles. It encompasses the journey taken, spreading positive messages grounded in faith and authenticity. Success is reflected in the life one has led, inspiring others selflessly, without seeking personal gain. Above all, success is about acquiring knowledge and pursuing education, whether it be in the field of law or medicine, by attending reputable institutions of learning.

~

Success, is about the person that you are, your intentions to succeed, and the will power, to go far. It's not about flaunting material possessions like diamond rings and making others feel left out while you move on to the next big thing. True success lies in believing in yourself and having the faith to proceed, even when faced with challenges along the way. It's about working harder to achieve your goals and create wealth for yourself. Success is also about living out all your dreams, looking past difficulties with determination, and realizing that the world is not as daunting as it may initially appear.

Death

Time: 22:07
Date: 09/02/24

I ponder the mysteries of what lies beyond,
When our mortal bodies cease to respond.
Does the soul ascend to heavenly heights,
Or is it consumed by eternal nights?

~

In search of answers, we yearn to learn,
To unravel the secrets that death may churn.
But alas, no one truly knows for sure,
What fate awaits us when life's curtain does obscure.

~

We grasp at fragments of ancient lore,
Seeking solace in tales from days of yore.
Yet the truth remains elusive and unclear,
Leaving us in a state of constant fear.

~

But perhaps it is not for us to know,
The grand design that orchestrates this show.
For life's true purpose lies in how we live,
The love we give and how we forgive.

~

So let us embrace each precious breath,
And cherish the moments before our last step.
For in the end, it matters not what comes after death,
But rather how we lived and loved with every breath.

Prevail

In life, determination is key,
It's what separates the possible from the impossible, you see.
When faced with challenges that seem too tough,
It's your determination that helps you stay rough.

~

For those who prevail, it's not just luck,
It's the fire inside them that they constantly stoke.
They face setbacks and obstacles with unwavering will,
Knowing that through determination, they can fulfil.

~

So when life throws curveballs and knocks you down,
Remember to rise up and wear determination like a crown.
No matter how impossible things may seem,
With determination, you can turn them into a dream.

~

So let your determination guide you on your way,
And never let the impossible lead you astray.
Believe in yourself and keep pushing ahead,
With determination as your companion, success lies ahead.

~

And as they face the consequences, their spirits never fail,
For in their hearts they hold the strength to prevail.

You don't always need a plan, my friend,
Sometimes, just take a deep breath and let go,
The worries will transcend.
In this journey of life, trust is key,
Believing in yourself and in a higher power, you'll see.
~

When doubts begin to creep in your mind,
Remember that you're strong and capable, one of a kind.
Imagination is a powerful tool indeed,
It helps you navigate through challenges with speed.
~

Don't fret about what tomorrow may bring,
Live in the present moment and let your heart sing.
Breathe in the beauty of each passing day,
And trust that everything will fall into place along the way.
~

Let go of fear and embrace the unknown,
Have faith that you're never truly alone.
For when you release control and surrender with grace,
The universe conspires to guide you to your rightful place.
~

So breathe, trust, and learn to let go,
And watch as life's wonders continue to unfold.
When you learn to take a breath,
That's your way of saying, "I'm ready for this test."
When you trust in yourself and others too,
That's your way of saying, "I believe in what we can do."
~

But when you let go of fear and doubt,
That's your way of saying, "I'll figure it out."
And when success comes knocking at your door,

You'll realize that you were worth fighting for.

~

So remember to breathe, trust, and let go,
For in those moments, true growth will show.
With each step forward, you'll find your way,
And create a future brighter than any yesterday.

Temptation

Time: 22:23
Date: 09/02/24

Temptation will always come knocking at your door,
But remember, it's a test to see if you'll explore.

~

Stay strong in your convictions and hold steady,
For giving in will only leave you feeling unsteady.

~

The allure of vices may seem enticing,
But don't let them lead you astray, for they're not worth
sacrificing.

~

Resist the urge to indulge in what may harm,
And instead focus on staying true to your charm.

~

For every temptation that comes your way,
There's a greater reward waiting at the end of the day.

~

So choose wisely and stay on the right track,
Don't let temporary pleasures hold you back.

~

Keep your motivation burning bright,
And watch as you conquer each and every fight.

~

When faced with temptation, it's crucial to remember,
Life's path is not about surrender.
Though the allure may be strong,
Stay steadfast and prove yourself wrong.

~

For there will always be invitations,
To indulge in harmful sensations.
But don't let them pull you astray,
Stay true to your goals every single day.

~
Whether it's drugs or alcohol's allure,
Resist the urge, remain pure.
Don't let them lead you down a dark road,
Choose strength and watch your spirit unfold.

~
The journey won't be easy, that much is clear,
But remember, you have nothing to fear.
With determination as your guide,
You'll conquer all obstacles with pride.

~
So when faced with the temptation's call,
Remember that you're stronger than them all.
Stay focused, stay motivated, don't give in,
And watch as your life transforms from within.

~
In this journey of life, you'll face temptation,
But remember, it's your determination that will lead to
elevation.

~
Stay strong, resist the allure and stay true to your destination.

I am in Charge

Time: 09:34
Date: 10/02/24

I am in charge of my emotions,
And today, I choose to let go of any commotions.
~

I will not allow negativity to seep in,
Instead, I'll focus on the positivity that lies within.
~

I understand that life can be tough,
But I refuse to let it make me feel rough.
Instead, I will embrace togetherness and love,
And rise above any sadness that tries to shove.
~

I will fill the void of loneliness with laughter and joy,
And find solace in the moments that life employs.
~

To move forward, I must confess my sins,
And with tenderness, forgive myself and begin again.
~

I will work harder each day,
To pave my own path, come what may.
I won't settle for anything less than my best,
Because I know deep down, I am truly blessed.
~

Sometimes, I may feel a bit suppressed,
But by closing my eyes and taking a rest,
~

I can rejuvenate my spirit and find peace,
Knowing that life's challenges will eventually cease.
~

I am in Charge, the captain of my fate,
With every step I take, I conquer and create.
No longer bound by sorrow, I embrace joy's embrace, For I
hold the power to shape my own space.

I will strive for greatness, fueling my ambition's fire, Each challenge I face, I will rise higher and higher. No more dwelling on past mistakes or regrets, I am in Charge, and it's time to place new bets.

Intelligence

Time: 04:07
Date: 06/02/2024

Intelligence without ambition, is like a bird without wings,
It may appear impressive, but lacks the power to do great
things.

~

Intelligence is like a symphony, with many harmonious parts,
Without it, we are just puppets, controlled by life's darts.

~

For some, intelligence is a magnet, drawing others near,
But for others, it's a curse, causing them fear.
The sexiest man will open your legs,
But an intelligent man will open your mind and heart instead.

~

In this world, where ego rules and pride reigns supreme,
Being kind instead of right can be a beautiful dream.

~

We all need someone who speaks with an intelligent mind,
But even more so, someone with a patient heart that's kind.

Friendship

On this special day, I celebrate our bond,
A friendship so strong, like a magic wand.
Through ups and downs, we've stood side by side,
Together we've faced every high and low tide.

~

You are the sunshine on my darkest days,
With you, my dear friend, life is always a blaze.
We laugh, we cry, we share secrets untold,
In this beautiful friendship, we've found solid gold.

~

Through thick and thin, we've weathered the storm,
Our friendship's foundation is truly warm.
No matter the distance or time that goes by,
Our connection remains unbreakable and high.

~

Friendship like ours is a treasure so rare,
A gift to cherish beyond compare.
So here's to you, my dearest friend,
May our bond shine bright until the very end.

~

As time moves near and birthdays come and go,
Our friendship continues to flourish and grow.
I'm grateful for your presence in my life,
A true friend like you brings joy amidst strife.

~

So let's raise a toast to the years yet to come,
Filled with laughter, adventures, and endless fun.
Happy birthday once again to you, my dear friend,
May our friendship endure till the very end.

Something Meaningful

If you want to succeed as bad as you want to breathe,
Then you will become successful, believe.
Success is not just about fame and wealth,
It's about finding something meaningful for yourself.

~

You wake up each day with a clear plan in mind,
With determination and motivation, you grind.
But amidst the hustle, never forget,
To be grateful for every sunrise you've met.

~

As you journey through life's winding road,
You'll encounter people, some kind and some cold.
But remember to treat them all with respect,
For it's the mark of a person truly perfect.

~

Surround yourself with a strong team,
One that supports your dream.
Choose friends who uplift and inspire,
And leave behind those who only conspire.

~

In the pursuit of success, stay true to your core,
Let your values guide you forevermore.
With hard work and dedication, you'll find,
That success is within your grasp, so kind.

~

Don't let the critics get inside your head, for their judgment is
something they dread. Stay focused on what truly matters,
and ignore their meaningless chatter. Remember, it's your
journey to define, so keep your dreams close and let them
shine.

Respecting Sally

Time: 05:17
Date: 06/02/24

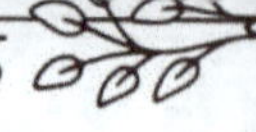

Respecting yourself may take a lot of courage,
It is not basic science but it will take a lot of knowledge.
But remember, dear friend, you deserve so much better,
Don't let negativity and pain be your love's fetter.

~

In this journey of life, you hold the key,
To unlock happiness and set yourself free.
Why stay in a relationship that brings you down?
Find the strength within to turn your life around.

~

You are worth more than the tears that you cry,
Don't let his hurtful words make your spirit die.
There's a world out there waiting for you to explore,
Where love and joy will knock on your door.

~

It's time to break free from this toxic rhyme,
And write a new poem with words that chime.
Choose happiness and let go of the past,
Embrace self-love and make it last.

~

Just like the single mother, determined and strong,
Resilient and focused, she knows where she belongs.
Not letting the absence of the father define her worth,
She's building a future that's destined for mirth.

~

So respecting yourself might be a little hard,
But once you embrace it, your spirit will never be marred.
No person on earth should make you feel blue,
Listen closely, Sally, for this message is for you.

~

You have immense potential and a bright path ahead,

With self-respect as your armor, you'll conquer with stead.
Believe in yourself and let your confidence flourish,
Embrace your worth and watch your dreams nourish.

Comfort Zone

Time: 05:40
Date: 06/02/24

It's time for you to step out of your comfort zone,
I don't want to hear your excuses,
I don't want to hear you moan,
All I ask is for you to disconnect from your phones,
Because once you do, a new world will be shown.

~

You claim you crave success, but you push me away,
You think you can achieve it all on your own someday,
But let me tell you, no one succeeds in that way,
To make it big, we need each other's support every day.

~

So if you want to act tough and go at it alone,
I'm here to remind you that together we've grown,
Success is not achieved by standing on a throne,
It takes collaboration and teamwork to truly be known.

~

I've been in this game, in and out,
Experiencing the highs and lows.
Nights spent on cold benches,
My only company being the stars that glow.
Wrapping myself up in a worn-out blanket,
Longing for a place to call my own.
Naively thinking I had it all figured out,
Believing I had already grown.

~

But deep inside, there was an emptiness,
A void I couldn't ignore.
Living like a shadow in the dark,
Unknown to the world's lore.
Every fiber of my being craved success,
Yearned for riches and fame,
Dreaming of sitting on the throne,

with fortune as my name.

~

So I toiled relentlessly,
Overcoming every obstacle that came my way.
Stepping over stones and hurdles,
Never letting them lead me astray.
Now I have the books filled with knowledge,
The cars that gleam and shine.
No longer needing to borrow or take out loans,
For success is truly mine.

~

In this journey called life,
I've learned that dreams can become reality.
With determination and perseverance,
we can achieve our own version of immortality.
So let us never give up on our aspirations or lose sight of our
goals.
For within each of us lies the power to create our own rhymes
and poems that touch souls.

Negativity

Time: 13:21
Date: 06/02/24

Don't expect a life filled with joy and glee,
If negativity is all you see.
Surround yourself with those who bring light,
And watch your world take flight.

~

In the company of negative souls,
You'll find yourself in deep, dark holes.
But if you choose to break free,
Positive changes you will soon see.

~

Choose uplifting friends who inspire,
And fuel your dreams with fire.
Leave behind the party scene,
Where drugs and needles intervene.

~

Embrace productivity, let your brain thrive,
And watch success into your life arrive.
No more dwelling in sadness and despair,
Instead, soar high like an eagle in the air.

~

Remember, my friend, negativity is evil,
So stay away from those who revel in smoking weed,
Popping pills, and drinking too much,
For their influence can be a dangerous touch.
Surround yourself with positivity's embrace,
And watch as your life falls into place.
With determination and a positive mind,
Success and happiness you will surely find.

~

Negativity may entice, with laughter and mirth,
But remember, dear friend, it's not always its true worth.

~
In this world of shadows and light,
Where trust can be shattered in the dead of night,
We must navigate with caution and care,
For not everyone's intentions are fair and square.

~

So hold your head high amidst the fray
Don't let their false masks lead you astray.

Persistence

Time: 23:51
Date: 06/02/24

Persistence is the key, my friend,
It's a quality that will never bend.
Through ups and downs, highs and lows,
You'll find strength in persistence that only grows.

~

Dedication and determination are at your core,
They're the fuel that keeps you going for more.
No matter the obstacles or how far the goal,
Your unwavering persistence will take its toll.

~

It's natural to feel afraid along the way,
But remember, consistency will never lead you astray.
Keep pushing forward with all your might,
And soon you'll see your dreams take flight.

~

The world may change and people may shift,
But your persistence will always remain a gift.
When you need support, don't hesitate to ask,
But never give up on your dreams; stay steadfast.

Ambitions

Look deep within, at your reflection's glare,
The one who meets your eyes, your only rival there.
Let ambition ignite, let it burn bright and strong,
For it is the driving force that propels you along.

~

Ambition pulses through your veins, a vital fire,
Fueling your efforts, pushing you higher.
Embrace the struggle, don't fear the pain,
For with each challenge faced, you'll surely gain.

~

Ambition is the spark that lights up your soul,
It gives purpose and meaning, making you whole.
Through thick and thin, it fuels your fight,
Guiding you towards the radiant light.

~

Persistence is the key to unlock success,
Working harder than anyone else, no need for rest.
With passion as your compass, strength as your guide,
You'll uncover secrets that others can't hide.

~

Without ambition, our dreams remain mere fantasies,
Empty vessels drifting on life's stormy seas.
So hold onto that drive, that burning desire,
Let ambition be the fuel that takes you higher.

It's Okay

It's okay if you didn't have a silver spoon in your mouth,
Just believe in yourself and let your passion shout.
It's okay if life has thrown you some curveballs,
Keep pushing forward and standing tall.

~

It's okay if you come from a small town or a big city,
Your potential knows no boundaries,
So embrace the nitty-gritty.

~

It's okay if people doubt your abilities and skills,
Prove them wrong and show them what you can fulfill.
It's okay to face obstacles along the way,
They are just stepping stones to a brighter day.
It's okay to stumble and fall,
Just remember to rise up and give it your all.

~

It's okay to dream big and aim high,
With determination and hard work, you'll reach the sky.
And it's alright to believe in the power of dreams,
To have that spark within you that constantly beams.
Even if they say your aspirations are too high,
Don't let their doubts and negativity make you sigh.

~

It's okay to hold onto hope, no matter how small,
Because sometimes, it's the tiniest flame that can ignite it all.

~

Keep pushing forward, even when the path seems unclear,
For perseverance and determination will always steer.
So don't be discouraged by those who judge and scorn,
Believe in yourself, for it's your dreams that were born.

Imma

Time: 12:32
Date: 07/02/24

They say the sky is the limit,
But I see beyond its vast expanse,
Imma soar through the heavens, defying gravity's dance.
With determination as my guide, I'll conquer every hurdle,
Imma unleash my potential, my dreams unfurl.

~

In my stylish attire, I'll make a statement that's bold,
Imma don my favourite hat, a story waiting to be told.
No time for idle chit-chat, success is calling my name,
Imma seize every opportunity, ignite my own flame.

~

I won't be deterred by self-doubt or societal norms,
Imma break free from limitations, weather any storms.
For those who think they're overweight or not enough,
Imma encourage self-love and confidence, that's the stuff.

~

Though I may not possess nine lives like a feline creature,
Imma explore new horizons, become an adventurer.
One day when I wake up, there'll be no need to spat,
For I'll have left an indelible mark, accomplishments stacked.

~

So let the world witness my journey unfold with grace,
Imma embrace challenges and emerge in first place.
With unwavering belief and unwavering resolve,
Imma write my own destiny, problems to solve.

I Remain

Time: 17:42
Date: 09/02/24

If you go first, and I remain,
I will carry your laughter, like a sweet refrain.
~
If you go, and I remain,
I'll cherish our moments, like drops in the rain.
~
If you go first, and I remain,
I'll hold onto your touch, like a lingering flame.
~
If you go, and I remain,
I'll keep your smile alive, in every frame.
~
If you go first, and I remain,
I'll write our story, in verses untamed.
~
If you go, and I remain,
I'll whisper your name, in the wind's gentle claim.
~
If you go first, and I remain,
I'll keep our love blooming, through seasons of strain.
~
If you go, and I remain,
I'll find solace in memories we've yet to attain.
~
If you go first, and I remain,
I'll honour our love, with a heart that won't wane.
~
If you go, and I remain,
I'll hold onto our love's essence, forever ingrained.

Your love, like a symphony, plays a sweet tune,
It echoes in my heart and makes me swoon.
From the moment we met, I was hooked,
But now without you, my life feels overlooked.

~

I reach out to the heavens above,
Praying for a sign of your love.
Every night, I whisper your name,
Hoping that somehow you'll feel the same.

~

But as the days pass by, I start to fear,
That your love may never reappear.
I'm lost without you, my guiding light,
And every day feels like an endless night.

~

I search for you in every place,
Yearning to see your familiar face.
Without you, life feels incomplete,
And my heart longs for our love to meet.

~

Your love, a gift I cherished and adored,
But now my heart is broken, shattered, and sore.
They say time heals all wounds, helps hearts to mend,
But how can I move on when you're no longer my friend?
I try to live life and find joy in each day,
But your absence lingers, casting shadows in my way.
The world beckons me with its wonders untold,
Yet without you by my side, it feels empty and cold.

~

I thought love would bring only happiness and delight,
But now it feels like a never-ending fight.

I'm sorry, I can't let go of what we once had,
For the memories of us make my heart feel so sad.

~

I yearn for the days when our love was so pure,
When our souls intertwined and our connection was sure.
But now I'm left with a void that cannot be filled,
And the pain of losing you remains deeply instilled.

The Wind 2

I can hear the wind, as it whispers in my ear,
Its gentle touch brings solace, and calms my inner fear.
~

The thunder roars above, with a powerful might,
But I find comfort in the wind's soothing flight.
~

It carries away my pain, with every gust that blows,
Leaving behind a sense of peace, that only nature knows.
~

The wind dances through the trees, creating a symphony,
Its melodies intertwine, like a beautiful harmony.
~

With each breath I take, I feel the wind's embrace,
It carries me to a tranquil state, where troubles are erased.
~

In its invisible arms, I find strength and release,
As the wind whispers secrets of serenity and inner peace.
~

No storm can break me, when the wind is by my side,
For it carries me through darkness, with unwavering stride.
~

So I embrace the wind's presence, with gratitude and grace,
For it heals my soul and brings a smile to my face.

Stay away from those who bring you down,
Negative people, the biggest clowns.
They thrive on spreading doubt and fear,
Their toxic energy is so clear.

~

They drain your motivation and drive,
Leaving you feeling barely alive.
Their words pierce through like sharp knives,
Destroying dreams and crushing lives.

~

Their lies are like a well-oiled machine,
Fueling negativity, so obscene.
They'll break you until you're just bones,
Leaving you feeling all alone.

~

Like the devil, they sow seeds of strife,
Causing trouble and chaos in life.
But remember, their power is not eternal,
Don't let their negativity be your internal.

~

Surround yourself with positivity and light,
Shine bright and keep up the good fight.
For negative people may try to meddle,
But your dreams and goals will always be your medal.

~

Beware of those who bring you down,
Negative people, they wear a frown.
They'll drain your energy, like a leech,
Stay away from them, practice what you preach.

~

Embrace the ones who uplift and inspire,

With them by your side, you'll reach higher.
Leave behind the negativity and its noise,
For in the end, it's your happiness you should rejoice.

Surround Yourself

Time: 05:53

Date: 06/02/24

Surround yourself with the dreamers and the doers,
The believers and the thinkers,
But, most of all, surround yourself with, YOU!

~

You have the TALENT to succeed;
You're not faithless, GO, proceed,
Never be aimless, and you will not bleed,
Just be painless, even when life is not guaranteed.

~

When you believe in yourself,
you will amount to something great.
You're a dreamer and a doer, so just forget about the hate.

~

Forget about the diamonds and the babies, just have faith,
If you believe in yourself, you could become the next
president of the United States.

~

So write your own story, make it unique,
With every word you speak, let your voice peak.
Embrace the power within you to rhyme,
Let your thoughts flow like poetry in time.
Don't hold back your dreams or limit their scope,
Believe in yourself and have unwavering hope.
For in this world of endless possibilities,
You are the author of your own destinies.

~

Through every trial and every test,
Stand tall and face them with your best.
For you possess the strength to overcome,
And turn every challenge into a stepping stone.

~

So surround yourself with positivity and cheer,
And let your dreams guide you through any fear.
Remember that success starts from within,
With belief in yourself, victory will begin.

In the depths of her soul, her feelings reside,
A tangled mess of emotions she cannot hide.
Behind closed doors, a world so dark and cruel,
She's been through beatings, crying, and more than she can
bear.

~

Hope slowly fades away, leaving her broken and shattered,
Her once youthful beauty now seems tattered.
Uncertainty engulfs her, causing her to feel lost,
She seeks solace in the bottle, at any cost.

~

Her heart is heavy, her mind a chaotic mess,
Every sip she takes brings temporary forgetfulness.
But deep down inside, she knows she's a mother,
And this destructive path can no longer smother.

~

With determination rising within her core,
She refuses to tolerate this life anymore.
No longer will she be trapped in this twisted game,
It's time to break free and reclaim her name.

~

Her feelings, a tumultuous sea,
Swirl within her, so wild and free.
With every glance at her daughter's face,
She sees the years, the time's swift pace.
Regret fills her heart, like a heavy stone,
If only she had known, if only she had known.
But life's choices were made, paths were set,
And now she longs for a chance to reset.

~

She yearns for a connection, a bridge to build,
To mend the wounds that time has filled.
Her feelings consume her, day and night,
Aching for reconciliation, longing for things to be right.

~

But deep down inside, she knows the truth,
That healing takes time and patience, in sooth.
So she waits and hopes, with bated breath,
That one day they'll find their love's sweet depth.

Homelessness

Time: 13:44
Date: 07/02/24

Did you know that homelessness is a plight?
A struggle faced by many, day and night.
No shelter to shield them from the cold,
Their stories of hardship remain untold.

~

They yearn for food, for a sip of water,
While we take these basic needs for granted, like fodder.
Their lives are filled with immense sadness,
While we dwell on trivial matters, blinded by our own madness.

~

You say you're grateful, but do you truly understand?
The privilege you possess at your command.
With a family by your side, love and support abound,
Yet you lack the ability to forgive and be unbound.

~

Out there, their bodies bear the scars of brokenness,
But in their hearts, they still hold onto hopefulness.
Oh dear God, in your grace and righteousness,
Shower them with your love and tenderness.

~

In a world plagued by homelessness,
We must rise above and address,
The needs of those who suffer in despair,
With compassion and kindness, let's show we care.

~

Forget the judgment, forget the blame,
Let's strive to end this cycle of shame,
By offering support, a helping hand,
Together, we can help them stand.

~

No longer should they feel defenceless,
Let's provide them with hope and tenderness,
For in their hearts, dreams still reside,
With our support, their spirits will rise.

~

So let us fight this battle with love and grace,
Embracing empathy, leaving no trace,
Of prejudice or discrimination, we say no more,
Let's open our hearts, let kindness pour.

Stop! Don't dwell on the negative thoughts,
Let's shift our focus to what life has brought.
Instead of worrying about what could go wrong,
Let's embrace the possibilities and sing a joyful song.

~

Negativity may bite and leave a painful mark,
But we have the power to ignite a positive spark.
Instead of letting it wriggle and move in our minds,
Let's choose optimism and leave negativity behind.

~

Think not about the could have beens or the probabilities,
For they only bring doubt and uncertainties.
Instead, let's envision all the things that can go right,
And watch as positivity takes flight.

~

Embrace the mights, the potentials yet untold,
For in them lies a future waiting to unfold.
Banish the doubts, let them scatter like dust,
And trust that positivity is what we must thrust.

~

So let go of negativity's grip on your soul,
And allow positivity to take control.
Think not of what might go amiss,
But focus on all the joys and bliss.

Cheaters Choice

Losing you, has been my greatest ever achievement,
A bittersweet triumph, a sigh of relief.
But in the aftermath of our love's bereavement,
I discovered a world filled with disbelief.

~

For once, I wore the crown of a cheater,
A master manipulator, playing games with hearts.
But now I see the error of my ways clearer,
Caught in a web of lies, torn apart.

~

Locked up in my own prison of regret,
My brain shuts down, overwhelmed by shame.
No longer able to pretend or forget,
I bear the burden of my cheaters' name.

~

You saw every girl as a pawn in your game,
Abusing their trust, using them for your gain.
Now they're locked away in sorrow and shame,
Only to be discarded like the remnants of rain.

~

Cheaters Choice, heed my voice,
Beware of those who play with poise,
Not all girls are what they seem,
Some may be schemers, masters of the scheme.
Before you commit, take a moment to reflect,
Consider wisely, don't be circumspect.
Your money's value should not be squandered,
By those who cheat and leave you pondered.
So be cautious in your selection,
Choose wisely, avoid deception.

Behind Her Lipstick

Time: 14:34
Date: 07/02/24

Behind her lipstick, a story untold,
A tale of strength and courage, yet to unfold.
Her smile may be pretty, but it hides the pain,
A past filled with struggles, hard to explain.

~

In her younger days, a father so cruel,
Using a screw as a tool to fuel,
His anger and frustration, leaving scars behind,
But she survived and blossomed, against all odds aligned.

~

At just fifteen, she sought solace in glue,
Escaping reality, searching for something new.
But through it all, her spirit remained strong,
Finding beauty in the world, even when things went wrong.

~

Behind her lipstick lies a journey of resilience,
A testament to her inner brilliance.
So let's not judge by appearances alone,
For there's always more to someone than what is shown.

~

Her mummy chose the shade, a vibrant blue,
Little did they know, the battles she'd go through.
With glue in her hands, she faced life's trials,
Taking care of her brother, while hiding her smiles.
The world couldn't see the strength in her eyes,
They judged her appearance, without knowing her highs.

~

But as I stand here, witnessing her grace,
I see the beauty beneath, in every trace.
To this stranger, you're not alone in your strife,
Together we'll conquer, and create a new life.

So wipe away those tears and keep your head high,
Your struggles will fade, like a distant goodbye.
Behind that lipstick lies a warrior's soul,
Ready to face anything that comes and make it whole.

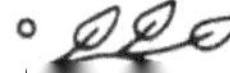

Foundation

Difficult roads only lead to beautiful destinations,
Stay strong and be focused, let's build a foundation.
~

No need to fret, my friend, for jobless days,
Let's fill those applications, pave new ways.
Though it may seem tough, frustration in the air,
Release those worries, success is yours to bear.
~

Avoid the temptations, the vices that bind,
Invest your time wisely and leave them behind.
Calculate your worth, let money flow your way,
Embrace your talents, prove them all wrong today.
~

Breathe in the possibilities, stretch beyond doubt,
Shrug off accusations with a confident shout.
You're destined for greatness, let haters see,
Your demonstration of brilliance is meant to be.
~

In this journey of life, success is your destination,
But remember, my friend,
It requires dedication and determination,
Like a skyscraper rising high with strong foundation,
You'll reach the top, no matter the situation.
~

Don't rush, for Rome wasn't built in a day,
There may be challenges along the way,
But keep pushing forward without delay,
And you'll achieve your dreams, come what may.
~

Let the haters laugh and doubt your aspiration,
Their words are mere illusions, a false narration,

Stay focused on your goals with unwavering dedication,
And watch as you conquer with your solid foundation.

Drinking Mummy

Drinking Mummy, I see your pain,
In the bottles of alcohol, you drown again.
But what about me, your little one?
Yearning for your love, needing to feel the sun.

~

Your anger consumes you, it's tearing us apart,
These meaningless fights, breaking my fragile heart.
When will you realize, the damage that you do?
Drinking every night, neglecting me and you.

~

You're trapped in this cycle, unable to break free,
Thinking you're always right, blinded by what you see.
But the truth is clear, like a beacon in the night,
Alcohol won't bring happiness or make things right.

~

Look at yourself, so small and lost in your own plight,
Believing that drinking makes you a delight.
But dear Mummy, it's time to face reality,
Your addiction is stealing your true identity.

~

You are more than just a woman lost in the night,
You have the strength within to make things right.
So put down the bottle and hold me tight,
Together we can find a new path in the light.

More Open

She said, "I am down in the dumps, and I am broken,
But deep within, a spark of hope has awoken.
I want to break free from this cycle of despair,
To find strength within myself and repair.

~

"More open to love, to joy, to light,
No longer burdened by the darkness of night.
I will rise above the pain and the strife,
Embracing a new chapter, a fresh lease on life.

~

"For too long, my dreams have been suppressed,
But now I'll pursue them with relentless zest.
No longer defined by my past's cruel token, I'll write a new
story, one that's more open."

~

More open in our hearts and minds,
To the struggles and hardships that we find,
For every woman who's been silenced and oppressed,
We'll speak up and fight for their rights, no less.

~

No more hiding behind smiles that deceive,
It's time to stand tall, not willing to leave,
The path of justice and equality,
Where every voice is heard with clarity.
Together, we'll break free from the chains,
Empowering women, unbound by constraints,
With courage and strength, we'll pave the way,
To a future where all women have their say.

~

So let us be more open, embrace the call,
To dismantle injustice once and for all,

Through words that rhyme, we'll make our stand,
For a world where women's voices expand.

A Good Parent

A good parent is one who's always connecting,
Through words and actions, they're constantly affecting.
They understand the power of their speech,
And use it wisely in their child's reach.

~

They know that bonds are built on trust,
Not just through substances that may combust.
A good parent teaches respect and love,
Guiding their child from high above.

~

But sometimes, even the best may feel unsure,
Seeking guidance from a higher power.
They acknowledge their own limitations,
And ask for divine intervention in their situations.

~

Life can be tough, and children need protecting,
A good parent knows the importance of detecting.
They reflect on their actions, seeking self-improvement,
For they understand the impact of their every movement.

~

So let us strive to be good parents each day,
Nurturing our children in every possible way.
With love, understanding, and constant connection,
We can raise them to be pillars of affection.

Women

Time: 5:16
Date: 07/02/24

Women, they possess a wisdom untold, Their intelligence
shines bright, never old. With minds sharp and quick as a
dart, They navigate life with grace and art.

~

Observing from afar, they silently think,
Analyzing every move, every blink.
But beware, for if you err again,
They'll make you feel small, like mice in a den.

~

Some may shed tears or sink in despair,
Yet they'll rise stronger, mending with care.
Slowly they'll step forward, on the edge,
Resilient and determined, refusing to pledge.

~

So perhaps it's time to reconsider your view,
For women are there to support and pursue.
They'll cook and clean with love in their heart,
But play with their emotions, and you'll fall apart.

There is no elevator to success,
You have to take the stairs,
Life is a journey, so you have to wipe away those tears.
~

I know that it's been difficult, I have seen it all these years,
All the struggles, all the hardship, YES!
They've murdered all your peers.
~

But life doesn't end there,
You have to keep your head held high,
Fight those battles and believe in yourself;
GO! Give the world a try.
~

As long as you are living, and not just some bones that has
Just died, life is a journey, go, hop on, give it a try.
~

Embrace the challenges that come your way,
For they shape you and make you stronger each day.
~

Rise above the doubts and fears in your mind,
With determination and perseverance, success you will find.
Though the path may be steep and filled with strife,
Keep pushing forward, for this is your life.
~

Believe in yourself and trust your own worth,
And watch as your dreams begin to unearth.
~

Remember, success doesn't come overnight,
It's through hard work and effort that you'll reach new
heights.

She said, with a heavy heart,
"I can't bear it anymore, we must part.
You're a bad mother, drowning in despair,
Leaving me to pick up the pieces, it's just not fair.

~

Your drinking has torn us apart,
Leaving scars on my soul and breaking my heart.
I've tried to help you, to make you see,
But all you do is drown in a sea of misery.

~

I cannot continue this toxic dance,
Where your drunkenness takes its chance.
It's time for me to break free,
To find a life where happiness can be.

~

I'll leave you now, to your bottle of sorrow,
For I can no longer bear the pain that follows.
You'll drink and drink until you're numb,
But remember, your actions have consequences to come.

~

I'll find strength in myself, in my own way,
To heal the wounds caused by your disarray.
No longer will I be burdened by your strife,
For I deserve a better life."

What about me, she said with a sigh,
Yearning for attention, asking why,
Her mother consumed by her own pain,
Unable to see her daughter's strain.

~

Her father gone, leaving a void,
Leaving her alone, feeling destroyed,
She longed for protection and support,
But instead, all she got was retort.

~

No family to turn to, no one to call,
Feeling trapped, feeling small,
All she wanted was to break free,
To find a love that would never flee.

~

She dreamed of a future so bright,
A husband who would hold her tight,
Someone who would never forsake,
And bring an end to the heartache.

~

What about me, you never thought to ask,
As I carried the weight of our relationship's task.
Now that I'm gone, you'll finally see,
The consequences of neglecting me.

Time: 18:00
Date: 09/02/24

Better Life

In the pursuit of a better life, I strive every day,
To overcome obstacles and find my own way.
Money may tempt, but it won't define me,
For the values instilled by those who raised me.

~

Growing up in a world filled with slavery's pain,
I reflect on it often, seeking to maintain,
The strength to rise above, to not be held back,
My daddy's words echo, "Don't worry, stay on track."

~

I work hard to earn my living,
And ensure that it's fulfilling.
No matter where I go or what I achieve,
I won't forget where I come from, that I believe.

~

May the Lord watch over me, each step of the way,
Guiding and protecting me, come what may.
With gratitude in my heart, I'll forever sing his praise,
As I navigate life's journey, through its twists and maze.

You can't kill someone, who already has dead emotions.
Someone who's heart is trapped, shattered and thrown into
the ocean.
~

You cannot turn around and say "you've lost your devotion",
When in reality, your love is a powerful potion.
~

She adores you,
She worries,
Why do you provoke such commotion?
~

When you dismiss the signs,
Expect an explosive motion.
~

If you truly cherish her, observe her body's motions,
Invest time and affection, like applying love lotion.
~

Devotion, a powerful emotion that binds,
A love so strong, it echoes through our minds.
But how can one claim to take it away,
When love's fire burns brighter every day?
~

In the depths of her heart, emotions may be dead,
But devotion lingers, like a flame in her head.
Her shattered soul, tossed into the sea,
Yet still she loves you, without any plea.
~

She stirs up commotion, for love's sake,
Hoping you'll notice and your heart will wake.
But if you ignore the signs and let her go,
The explosion of pain is all you'll know.

~

So instead of turning away from her devotion,
Take the time to understand her body's motion.
With love as your lotion, heal her wounded soul,
And watch as your bond grows stronger than coal.

~

With devotion, she offers her heart's affection,
But tearing it apart is not the right direction.
For when you lift her up, only to break her down,
Trust diminishes and love starts to drown.
In a woman's mind, love and lust intertwine,
But too much pain can make mistrust align.
So handle her heart with gentle care,
And let your love for her always be fair.

Winners

Winners, they don't always have it easy,
They face challenges and obstacles that make them queasy.
But what sets them apart is their unwavering will,
To keep pushing forward, to never stand still.

~

They understand that failure is part of the game,
It's not a reason to hang their heads in shame.
Mistakes are just proof that they're trying harder,
Learning from each stumble and becoming smarter.

~

In this journey, they don't give up on their dreams,
Even when life throws them illness or extreme themes.
They fight through the pain, with determination and might,
Refusing to let anything dim their inner light.

~

Some may choose the path of destruction and despair,
Thinking that shortcuts and wrongdoings are fair.
But winners know better, they rise above the rest,
Choosing integrity and resilience as their best.

~

So if you find yourself at a crossroads too,
Remember what winners do, and you can make it through.
Embrace your failures, learn from every fall,
And soon enough, success will come knocking on your wall.

The Seeds

Time: 17:05
Date: 09/02/24

The seeds that you plant today have a great potential to
Harvest in many years to come,
If you only think about where you are going,
And what you are doing wrong.

~

Stop that noise, you are strong.
I see depression, I see pain, but they are wrong,
You will overcome this feeling, use your faith, go sing your
songs.

~

I knew all along,
You will achieve amazing things, because you are strong.

~

You're determined, You're educated,
You'll be off to Hong Kong.

~

And when the devil tries to win, just laugh and say, you are
wrong. I'm a woman of Christ, and today is how my life
began.

~

Believe in yourself and trust your intuition,
For within lies the power of manifestation.
Plant positive thoughts and nurture them with care,
For they will grow into dreams beyond compare.

~

Embrace the challenges that come your way,
They are opportunities in disguise every day.

~

Turn setbacks into stepping stones for success,
And watch as your life becomes truly blessed.

~

Stay focused on your goals and never lose sight,
With perseverance and determination, you'll reach new heights.

~

So don't be discouraged by what may seem tough,
Remember that the seeds you sow will be enough.

~

In due time, they'll bloom into a beautiful sight,
And all your efforts will shine with radiant light.

Advice

Time: 17:30
Date: 09/02/24

In this journey called life, I offer my advice,
But remember, it's your choice to be wise.

~

Take heed and listen to the words I speak,
For in them lies the knowledge you seek.

~

Embrace the lessons that come your way,
They'll guide you through each passing day.

~

But don't just pretend or put on a show,
Authenticity is key, let your true self glow.

~

When faced with decisions, stay strong and clear,
Trust yourself, and have no fear.

~

And when frustration knocks at your door,
Remember, you have the power to soar.

~

So take a moment to pause and reflect,
Make changes, big or small, with respect.

~

For in this beautiful journey we undertake,
It's up to you to shape your own fate.

Tough times don't last, that's what they say,
But it can be hard to keep the doubts at bay.
Life's challenges test us, day after day,
But with determination, we'll find our own way.

~

In this battle called life, we may stumble and fall,
But we'll rise again, standing tall.
Though it kicks us down, until we're feeling blue,
We won't give up, because we know what we can do.

~

When tough times mock us and try to deter,
We push forward, fueled by our inner fire.
We won't let their words break our spirit or sway,
For we are strong enough to forge our own way.

~

So don't let tough times bring you down,
Embrace hardship as part of your life's crown.
Work a little harder, push through the strife,
And soon you'll be savoring the sweet taste of life.

Promises

Why do some people never know how to keep their
promises? It's a question that truly baffles and gnaws.
To make a pledge and then break it with ease,
Leaves others feeling hurt, deceived, and displeased.

~

But let us not dwell on those who deceive,
Instead, focus on the ones who believe.
For promises made with genuine intent,
Can bring about trust and contentment.

~

To be honest is the key, my dear friend,
A trait that will never fail or bend.
So let us strive to always stay true,
In our words and actions, in all that we do.

~

And remember, promises are not to be taken lightly,
They hold immense power, if used rightly.
So let us cherish them and honour our word,
For a promise kept is a beautiful accord.

Step into the light, embrace the day,
Are you ready to seize it, come what may?
With a heart full of courage and a mind so keen,
You are ready to conquer, to fulfill your dreams.
~

No more hesitations, no more doubts,
It's time to break free from those inner shouts.
Embrace your uniqueness, let it shine bright,
For you are capable of reaching new heights.
~

Leave behind the blame and the heavy load,
Choose forgiveness and lighten your road.
No longer dwelling on what could have been,
Focus on the present and let the past be seen.
~

So let's take a moment, just you and me,
To reflect on our journey and all that we can be.
With determination in our souls and fire in our eyes,
We are ready to face any challenge that lies.
~

Together we stand, united as one,
Ready to face whatever may come.
For we are humans, strong and steady,
And together, Eddie, we are truly ready.

Angel Dust

I can see your lies, like a cloud of Angel Dust,
Your deceit and betrayal, in my heart it thrust.
But I rise above, with strength and resilience,
No longer bound by your false brilliance.

~

I loved you deeply, but it was all a facade,
Now I see the truth, no longer feel awed.
Your fantasies and desires, they were just a ruse,
Leaving scars on my soul, like painful bruises.

~

But I've moved on, left the past behind,
Found someone who cherishes me, a love that's kind.
No longer trapped in your web of deceit,
I've found happiness again, in love's sweet retreat.

~

So let the fairy dust settle, let it fade away,
For I am stronger now, come what may.
No more lies or cheating to make me disgust,
I've embraced the truth and left behind the mistrust.

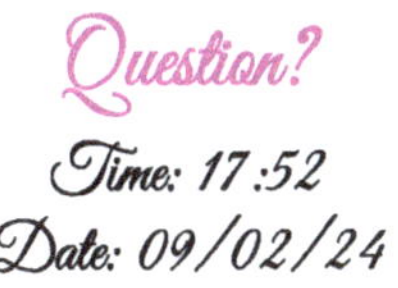

What is your aspiration?
What drives you to pursue?
What is it that ignites your fire?
What keeps your dreams anew?

~

What is it that inspires you?
What fuels your creative spark?
What is it that stirs your soul?
What leaves its vibrant mark?

~

What is it that challenges you?
What tests your strength and might?
What is it that fuels your passion?
What keeps you up at night?

~

What is it that fills your heart?
What brings you joy and bliss?
What is it that moves your spirit?
What moments do you reminisce?

~

When you ponder these queries, life's mysteries unfurl,
Revealing the essence, the truths that make your soul swirl.
With every question mark, a path to success is paved,
Unlocking potential, stretching beyond what you once craved.

~

The power of inquiry ignites the flames of thought,
Expanding horizons, revealing battles fought.
Through questions we find purpose, direction anew,
Unearthing the answers that lie within me and you.

~

So embrace the question mark, let it guide your way,
To a life filled with meaning, where doubts don't hold sway.
For in asking and seeking, we uncover our own bliss,
A journey of self-discovery, in questions lies our abyss.

The Abuser

Time: 21:55
Date: 09/02/24

The wounds you inflicted, deep and raw,
Left scars that I still feel, sore and raw.
But now the tables have turned, karma's law,
The abuser is now the one who withdraws.
~
You thought your power was never-ending,
But now you're the one who's bending.
Your actions have consequences, they're pending,
As your world crumbles, everything descending.
~
You used me like a pawn in your twisted game,
But now it's you who's filled with shame.
No longer will I bear the weight of your blame,
For I have found my voice, my own flame.
~
So go ahead and try to pretend,
That you didn't break me, that this isn't the end.
But deep down inside, you know you won't mend,
Because the abuser can never truly transcend.

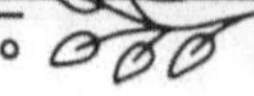

The Situation

Time: 18:08
Date: 09/02/24

In the midst of this situation,
A whirlwind of emotions, a combination.
Seeking solace in the doctor's care,
Questioning if it's the right path to bear.

~

Confusion lingers, love is unclear,
A puzzle to solve, no answers near.
Feelings of worthlessness begin to rise,
Words spoken hurt, tears fill her eyes.

~

Buried deep within, guilt takes its toll,
Hoping one day redemption will unfold.
Feeling lost in a world so vast,
Yearning for guidance that will last.

~

Amidst the pain and endless strife,
She reaches out for a better life.
For she is just a human, like me and you,
With a precious life growing within her too.

~

Through the ups and downs, thick and thin,
She believed she had strength within.
But now she's faced with doubt and fear,
Wondering if she can persevere.

~

In the situation of love's confusion,
Where hearts are tangled in an illusion,
She knows he's a player, that's clear,
But still, she holds him near.

~

He breaks her down, piece by piece,
Her soul lost, longing for release.
Her mother warns her, "Don't do it!",
But love blinds her, she can't see through it.
He uses and leaves her toothless,
Yet she loves him, in spite of the ruthlessness.
Only time will reveal the truth,
As this twisted love story continues to bruise.
~

But who is he to truly give a damn?
With no soul, he's just an empty sham.
Not just his pants lack substance and grace,
His mind too, leaving a void in its place.
~

The girls chase after his shallow charm,
Unaware that they're headed for harm.
This tale of love will surely end in disaster,
Leaving them broken and shattered.
~

The Situation he finds himself in is quite unique,
With no experience, he lives a life so sleek.
A player by nature, he knows how to thrive,
Turning his nights into moments that come alive.

Positive Message

Time: 23:35
Date: 06/02/23

Work hard in silence, and let success be your noise,
If you desire to make it in the future, you have to put away
your toys. Life isn't just about fun and games,
It's about determination and aiming for the highest aims.
Don't waste time on distractions and play,
Focus on your goals and seize the day.

~

Ambition is the fuel that drives us forward,
Motivation is what keeps us moving toward our dreams and
aspirations so grand, But determination is what helps us
withstand the challenges that come along our way.

~

So remember, don't shout or boast too loud,
Let your actions speak for themselves, proud.
The path to success is paved with hard work and grace,
So keep pushing forward at a steady pace.

Why are you feeling shy, my lovely lady fair?
Don't let their judgment affect the way you wear your hair.
Whether you're skinny or pretty, it doesn't really matter,
It's your confidence and inner beauty that will make them scatter.

~

So what if they think you don't fit in the city's scene?
You're unique and special, like a dazzling moonbeam.
Now don't be nervous, don't let doubts cloud your mind,
You're beautiful just the way you are, one of a kind.

~

If they try to bring you down, stand tall and stay strong,
Prove them wrong with your spirit, all day long.
And if shedding a few pounds can make you feel great,
Go ahead and do it, but remember, love yourself and your weight.

~

So pretty lady, embrace your individuality with pride,
Let their narrow-mindedness slide.
You are beautiful inside and out, that is true,
Never forget that, my dear, as I believe in you.

The Best

Time: 14:40
Date: 12/02/24

The best version of myself I will be,
In every endeavour, I'll strive to see,
Success and triumph, my constant decree,
From dawn till dusk, with unwavering glee.

~

I'll soar above challenges, like a bird in flight,
Breaking through barriers with all my might,
Leaving a mark that shines ever so bright,
A beacon of hope, guiding others to ignite.

~

With each step I take, I'll build my foundation strong,
Planting seeds of greatness, where they belong,
My name shall echo through the crowds, loud and long,
As the best in my field, where I truly belong.

~

No matter the odds or the limitations faced,
I'll push beyond boundaries and leave no trace,
For I am blessed with talents that can't be erased,
And as long as I live, success will embrace.

Until it's my turn, I will write.

With Love
Chavanese Wint